a GreenApples Guide

The ABCs & 123s of Breaking into Hollywood

A Personal Planner, Resource Guide and Journal for Aspiring Actors & Performing Artists

Fifth Edition

MS Blackwell

GROUND FLOOR PUBLISHING

Copyright © 2021 by MS Blackwell.
All rights reserved. No part of this book may be reproduced in any form or by any electronic or mechanical means, including information & digital storage and retrieval systems, without permission in writing from the publisher, except by a reviewer who may quote brief passages in a review.

Ground Floor Publishing
2005 Palo Verde Avenue, Suite 152
Los Angeles, California 90815

GFPBookz.com
GreenApplesGuide.com

Print and Digital distribution in the United States of America

Fifth edition released: January 2021.

Hello there,

You now have in your hands, ***The ABC's & 123's of Breaking into Hollywood***, a **GreenApples Guide,** which can be used to guide you through the intimidating, and on some level, arduous task of starting a career in the entertainment industry. You can also use the blank pages to jot down notes, your progress, people you meet, tape cards you collect along with other contacts and/or leads you may make on your career journey. This is your personal industry resource guide, journal, planner, etc., etc., etc. You can keep all the names (people, places (sites, email, etc.) and things) you come across on castings, sets and productions, or you find online while doing research. Anything else you come across.

This book has been broken into a few sections in order to make it easy to use. Section 1 is a checklist of things one would need to have if they want to break into the entertainment industry, from the ground up; Section 2 is a list of resources – the ABCs and 123s (literally) to help you break into the business; and Section 3 is a personal calendar and journal for you to chronicle your journey from aspiring to I MADE IT! Lastly, there is a Glossary of terms you will hear and experience as you begin working inside the industry. For instance, I've mentioned the "business" and "industry," both are words used within the entertainment industry to mean the entertainment industry.

My suggestion when using this book is to take it in one section at a time. Go over it as many times as you need to, as often as you need to, in order to complete the checklist in Section 1. Create notes and other materials utilizing the resources listed in Section 2 or the things you write down in Section 3. You can do it… and I hope this book helps you accomplish your dream of breaking into the Hollywood.

Best of Luck to You!

MS Blackwell
(*aka Coach Michelle*)

This Belongs To:

_____

Contact information:

Phone Number(s): (   )

Email(s):

Website(s):

Facebook:

Twitter:

Instagram:

Any other social media pages you have or plan to have:

Table of Contents

Section 1: Checklist for Breaking into Hollywood 7

Section 2: Resource Guide 12

Section 3: Personal Planner & Journal 68

Glossary 81

That's A Wrap! 98

SECTION 1:

Checklist for Breaking into Hollywood

First and foremost, when trying to break into any new career or business there are certain things you must possess or obtain in order to be successful. Breaking into Hollywood is no different. Here is a checklist of the 5 most important tools every Actor and/or Performing Artist **MUST** have or actively work to obtain:

- **Professional Headshots**
- **Resume**
- **Personal Website or Blog**
- **Social Media pages**
- **Demo Reel***

HEADSHOTS

First, what is a headshot and why are they important to an aspiring actor or performing artist? A *headshot* is a professional photograph (not a selfie or festive photo taken by family or friends during the holidays) used to create a personal image and/or brand one's self. Headshots usually focus on your upper body. Most actors do not include more than their head to shoulders in their professional headshot.

Second, a headshot conveys your professionalism. It is a way most actors make a first impression on casting professionals, potential agents or personal representation, etc., puts a face to your name. A good headshot gives an idea of how approachable you might be. It lets the onlooker know if you have the look they are seeking. If you met casting pros or agents during a showcase, performance, etc., your headshot will remind them of who you are. Try to keep your headshot current as it gives people an accurate idea of what you look like right now.

NOTE: if you cannot afford a professional photographer right now but in need of headshots, here are some tips for getting professional-ish photos to get you started. Again, STAY AWAY from using SELFIES as your headshot.

So, let's move on with your photo shoot. You want to either ask a friend if they will help you with the actual photography and camera, OR invest in a camera stand (i.e., tripod) to place your device on. Next you want to pick a location inside or outdoors. Wherever you decide please make sure the lighting is good. If you decide to shoot inside, choose a simple background, a plain wall, nothing too busy or cluttered to distract the casting directors, agents, etc. Also, if you are staying sides, it can't hurt to invest in additional lighting. Next, if you are using your phone be sure you have camera app, which will allow you to edit and/or retouch your photos. Be sure to clear up space on your phone.

Finally, you should give yourself at least two hours to shoot the photos and then a little more time should you want to retouch/edit your photos before adding or submitting them to your casting pages.

RESUME

What type of resume does an actor or performing artist need? There is a different between a general work-related resume and an acting **resume** is a resume specifically formatted for an actor who is seeking roles in movies, shows, stage or other productions within the entertainment industry. Acting related resume are unique in that they are specifically designed to accommodate or accompany an actor's headshot when submitting to casting professionals and/or producers of entertainment projects.

PERSONAL WEBSITE or BLOG

Why should an actor or performing artist have their own website? Most actors and artists know that we live in a digital era. Most people "*google*" or do an online search for any and everything (or anyone) they hear about. If someone mentions a new shop, eatery, movie, or clothing line you've never heard of before, what do you do… google it? And if you search up nearly everything you hear about, like me, and you can't find a website or blog posts for it, what are the chances you are going to just move on to something else? Think about it.

I am a writer, producer who also performs/acts-- a triple threat I like to call a Self Producing Performer, aka SPP, (I wrote a book about how to become a SPP. Want to read it? It should be released by mid 2021, visit GFPbookz.com or the publishers website at GroundFloorPublishing.com or you can always find it on Amazon)-- and as an SPP it was imperative that I have a personal website. It's MichelleBlackwell.com. You can read all about me and what it is I do.

The same thing goes when people are curious about an actor or artist. Potential casting pros and/or production companies *WILL* do an online search for you. So it's just good business to have your own professional [personal] website that shows up whenever someone searches for you. You can add content and photos or links to such, that you want people to see as a preventative of you and your previous work.

Your personal website or blog can be an important and useful marketing tool for your career. Ultimately it showcases who you are as an actor or artist and as a unique individual to casting directors, agents, and industry professionals. It's an opportunity to connect and network with people who might not know you or your work. That coupled with ways to get in contact you.

SOCIAL MEDIA

In this day and age, if someone needs to convince you that you need to have as many social media pages as you can put your name on then you are ions behind your fellow actors and artists. So, if you have not joined the digital age, at least for your career sake, please join in as soon as possible.

Social media is a great way to collect and keep in contact with your audience. At every stage of your career, the audience, writers, directors, producers, casting directors, and actors you work with can be your potential audience. So please connect and stay in touch with them via your social media pages, and organically grow your following as you grow.

DEMO REEL*

Lastly, let me explain why actors and performing artists need a good demo reel (known as a "*demo*" or "*reel*"). Casting directors and production company representatives, alike, use reels to get a look at you in living color. They get a sense of your acting abilities, talents and also gauge your on-camera presence and charisma. A great demo/reel can convince a casting director or production company rep to call you in for an audition or even cast you in a role without even auditioning. It can happen. So try to make your demo/reel as awesome as possible.

* *If you do not have any film or videos to create a demo/reel yet, no worries. Once you begin working on films, shows, stage, etc., you can start putting your demo/reel together. Just stay focused on breaking in and making your mark on the world!*

Wishing YOU all the best in your future career!

- **MS Blackwell** *(aka Coach Michelle)*

SECTION 2:
Resource Guide

Your list of entertainment industry resources starts here:

A   **Agent**
When a person decides to become a professional performer (no matter if it's as an actor, musical artist, comedian, broadcasting talent, etc.), there are so many things they need to take into consideration. One thing is obtaining an agent and/or personal manager. Talent can visit the Association of Talent Agents (at: agentassociation.com) or visit union websites, like SAG/AFTRA (find links in the ***U - Union*** section of this book) and/or casting websites like LA Casting or Actors Access (find links in the ***C - Casting*** section).

(Use this blank space to post/tape business cards, contact notes or create a vision board)

B Blog

Any on-camera talent who does not blog about themselves, project they are appearing in and/or their experiences within the entertainment industry, really needs to start! Here are some sources of where to go to get a blog started. Not all blogs are free so please be sure to thoroughly research to see if the blog site you are interested in charges to post your blog or not…

1. Blog.com
2. Blogger.com
3. eBlogger.com
4. Opendiary.com
5. Wordpress.com
6. Weebly.com
7. Livejournal.com
8. Blogster.com

(Use this blank space to post/tape business cards, contact notes or create a vision board)

| C | **Casting** |

Every star had to start somewhere, and many of them started off as a background player (aka "extra") in movies and television shows because everybody has got to eat. If you would rather get paid to work on actual movie and TV show sets, then check out the following casting companies who cast day players and even stand-in acting gigs…

1. Central Casting (centralcasting.com)   **6. IMDbPro** (imdb.com)

2. Actors Access (actorsaccess.com**)   7. Backstage** (backstage.com)

3. Casting Network (lacasting.com)

4. Project Casting (projectcasting.com)

5. Submission Bros casting (SubmissionBros.com)

(Use this blank space to post/tape business cards, contact notes or create a vision board)

D   Directories

You can find a lot of useful casting, employment and other production information through the pages of these directories. NOTE: this is not a comprehensive list, meaning these are just a few sources, the lines below this and all the other captions can and should be used to jot down other like sources for future reference. If you are not located in outside of California, do a search for entertainment directories in your city or state to see what comes up.

1. **The LA 411** (LA411.com)

2. **Hollywood Creative Directory** (search on amazon.com)

3. **Creative Handbook** (creativehandbook.com)

4. **Orange County Creative Directory** (TheOCcreativedirectory.com)

5. **San Diego Creative Directory** (sdcreativedirectory.com)

(Use this blank space to post/tape business cards, contact notes or create a vision board)

> ***E*** **Extra** (background) casting and **Call-in Services**
>
> If you are as lazy of a talent as I have been in the past, then after signing up with the like of Central Casting (listed in the "Casting" section) then you can sign up with a call-in service that will keep you working all the time. Here are a few companies that do this for you…
>
> 1. **CentralCasting(.com)**
> 2. **ExtrasManagement(.com)**
> 3. **BackgroundTalent(.net) Services**
> 4. **VirgoTalent(.com)**
> 5. **Commercial-Extras(.com)**

(Use this blank space to post/tape business cards, contact notes or create a vision board)

F   Facebook.com and **Instagram**

Simply put, every person who considers themselves "TALENT" needs to have a social network presence. So if you do not have a Facebook or Instagram page please go online to those sites and get yourself one as soon as possible! They help promote yourself and the projects you can be seen in. Very important tools.

(Use this blank space to post/tape business cards, contact notes or create a vision board)

G is for Grind…

Grind is to hustle what money is to spend… a must have! You must grind out or hustle at the career you want -- or face the reality that it may never happen! Bottom line is, the harder you work and the more you believe in yourself the greater your reward… (Just a little unsolicited advice).

(Use this blank space to post/tape business cards, contact notes or create a vision board)

| *H* | **Housing** |

If you are new to California ("Hollywood") or are planning to move here, then you are going to need to find a place to live. Now there are lots of sites online that you can go to find place to live if you are moving. Wherever you decide to move PLEASE make sure you thoroughly check out the space to make sure it's legit before giving your money. Also, the worldwide database Apartments.com is a great resource.

(Use this blank space to post/tape business cards, contact notes or create a vision board)

| *I* | **IMDB** |

Once you have a few credits under your belt you may want to make sure those credits are displayed on the database IMDB (the Internet Movies Database). You can even purchase your own IMDB page on their IMDBpro site, which leads to the main IMDB site. Check into it at IMDB.com or IMDbPro.com.

(Use this blank space to post/tape business cards, contact notes or create a vision board)

J **Jobs**

Finding a gig that will pay the bills while you are pursuing your Hollywood career? Then here are a few places to go to find out if there are jobs available now:

1. Indeed.com
2. Staffmeup.com
3. EntertainmentCareers.net
4. Mandy.com
5. Showbizjobs.com
6. Blackjobs.com

(Use this blank space to post/tape business cards, contact notes or create a vision board)

K is for *Keep* going…

If you keep going, and keep believe in yourself as well as your talent, and promise yourself you will never give up on your dream until you "make it"… success will definitely find you!! —said somebody

(Use this blank space to post/tape business cards, contact notes or create a vision board)

| *L* | **LinkedIn** |

Most people in the industry are *LinkedIn* and so should you. Go to Linkedin.com and sign-up. You will be asked for some basic background information such as your name, whatever contact info you wish to make public (email, message number, etc.) and some of your work experience and/or acting experience. This is a great way to network with people in your field.

(Use this blank space to post/tape business cards, contact notes or create a vision board)

M   *Marketing* using Social Media

When it comes to marketing yourself – take this very seriously! If you do not market yourself, on a constant basis, you will fade into obscurity. Here are a few places you will definitely want to attack BUT do not stop with just these sites:

1. Facebook.com
2. Instagram.com
3. ActorsConnect.com
4. Digg.com

5. Twitter.com
6. Stage32.com
7. Flickr.com
8. TalentSoup.com

(Use this blank space to post/tape business cards, contact notes or create a vision board)

N   **Networking via Social Media**

The same can be said about networking as marketing. This is an iatrical part of building your "brand" and getting yourself out there. So here are a few places on the web you can go but again, do not stop with just these. Make sure to keep your eye out for more as many places as you can to network yourself. Remember none of the sources in this book are absolute so please be sure to write down any networking opportunities you may hear during your acting classes, at the coffee shop, out at clubs, etc., so you can refer back to them at a later date.

1. Facebook.com
2. Intagram.com
3. Twitter.com
4. Delicious.com
5. Pinterest.com
6. Meetup.com

(Use this blank space to post/tape business cards, contact notes or create a vision board)

O is for *Opportunities...*

Opportunity only knocks on your door every once in a while. Do yourself a favor and stay mindful of this so you can open it the next time opportunity knocks! (a little more unsolicited advice)

(Use this blank space to post/tape business cards, contact notes or create a vision board)

| **P** | **Photos** |

Your image is everything. How you look and the image you portray can make or break your career. You want to give your look some careful consideration before you go out and take pictures (aka "headshots"). Photo sessions can run you anywhere from a hundred to a couple of hundred, maybe even thousands, depending on the photographer you choose.

To find the perfect photographer do a little research, either online or in local trade papers area to find quality photographers. Or better yet, check out some of the photos of fellow actor/ess you know and or like, to see if their photos are what you want, then ask for a referral to their photographer. Referrals are always best practices because you get to see the photographers "real" work before you contact them for a rate and/or appointment.

(Use this blank space to post/tape business cards, contact notes or create a vision board)

Q is for *Quitting*...

Okay listen... QUITTING is NOT an option!!! Keep pursuing your dreams because success could be right around the corner!! (another little piece of unsolicited advice)

(Use this blank space to post/tape business cards, contact notes or create a vision board)

R   Reels & Resumes

Once you start acting and performing in front of an audience or find a scene you really enjoy, you should capture it on tape (video) so that you can start building your reel as well as your resume. Listen, a reel is another way to showcase your talents and a resume is how you show your credits.

The best way to find someone to produce and/or edit your reel is word of mouth. In case you do not know anyone who can refer you then here are a couple of companies to help you get it started, if you reside in Los Angeles. Remember you should do a search for more companies who may meet your expectation. As for creating your resume, a sample is provided on the next page.

       1. Planetvideodemoreels.com   2. JigReelStudios.com

                      3. Theactorscompanyla.com

(Use this blank space to post/tape business cards, contact notes or create a vision board)

Sample Resume

PERFORMER'S NAME
UNION Affiliation

Height: Personal Contact Info
Weight: or Agency Contact
Eyes: *(note: some agencies will place their sticker here)*
Hair:

(Note: depending on what type of project you are going to be sending your resume to you may want to arrange and re-arrange your credits accordingly.)

FILM: *(list as many as you want)*
Project Title   [Your] Role   Prod. Company

TELEVISION: *(list as many as you want)*
Show Title   [Your] Role   Prod. Company

THEATRE: *(list as many as you want)*
Play   [Your] Role   Theatre/Company

WEB/INTERNET: *(list if you have)*
Project Title   [Your] Role   Prod. Company

COMMERCIALS/VOICE-OVER: Conflict available upon request.

TRAINING:
School/Facility   Technique Studied

SPECIAL SKILLS:
List dialects, extraordinary talents (singing, pole dancing, acrobatics, etc.) and any other skills you feel allow you to stand out in a crowd.

Example of A Professional Resume

Justine Tymme
SAG-AFTRA

Height: 5' 6"	(818) 555-7775
Weight: 125	Agents info here
Eyes: Brown	
Hair: Naturally Red	

FILM:

Treasure Island II	Supporting	Chase Ford Prods.
The Blame Game	Supporting	Carver Pictures

TELEVISION:

Scandal	Supporting	ShandaLand Prods.
Happily Divorced	Supporting	King Street Prods.

THEATRE:

Raisin In The Sun	Benetha	Chopin Theatre
Who's Afraid of Virginia Woolf	Honey	Talon Theatre

WEB/INTERNET:

Carter 'N Jonez	Jazmine Jonez	BDP Entertainment
Sweet Talk w/Dana Sweet	Dana Sweet	BDP Entertainment

COMMERCIALS: Available Upon Request.

TRAINING:

SMC Acting Class	Commercial Acting	Deb Thompson
Actor's Studios	Scene Study	Carl Brown

SPECIAL SKILLS:
Improv, Hosting, Teleprompter, Announcing/MC, Broadcasting/Sportscasting, Multiple accents, Writing and Producing (radio/TV/film); physical talent: Basketball, Horse riding, Skiing, Tennis, Golf, Boxing, Fencing, Golf, Running, Talking, Swimming, Jump Rope/Double Dutch, Badminton.

(Use this blank space to post/tape business cards, contact notes or create a vision board)

S Studying & Training

You must constantly hone your craft. Keep your chops well lubricated and the way you do that is to train. There are thousands of places to study in this town but I'm only going to list a few that I have personal knowledge of or have actually studied with myself. Many of the following training facilities are now offering online classes.

1. **The Acting Corps** (theActingCorps.com)

2. **Stella Adler Academy of Acting** (StellaAdler-la.com)

3. **The Actors Center** (ActorsCenter.com)

4. **The Beverly Hills Playhouse** (BHplayhouse.com)

5. **Hollywood Performance Academy** (HollywoodBackdoor.com)

(Use this blank space to post/tape business cards, contact notes or create a vision board)

T   Trade Magazines

Whenever you need to find something in the entertainment industry, no matter what it is you can always find it in the local trade papers. Whether you want to find

1. **Hollywood Reporter**(.com)
2. **Backstage**(.com)
3. **Production Hub**(.com)
4. **Variety**(.com)
5. **Billboard**(.com)

(Use this blank space to post/tape business cards, contact notes or create a vision board)

U **Unions**

At some point in your career, you will more than likely have to or may want to join a talent union. If you are already a member of a union, you know the pros & cons of union-hood. There are several entertainment unions and guilds to help protect the liberties of cast and crewmembers the stage and screen. Here are some of the known talent unions:

1. Screen Actors Guild (and **AFTRA**) sagaftra.org

2. Actors' Equity Association (AEA) actorsequity.org

3, Directors Guild of America (DGA) dga.org

4. Writers Guild of America (WGA) wga.org

5. Producers Guild of America (PGA) producersguild.org

(Use this blank space to post/tape business cards, contact notes or create a vision board)

V **Vlog (video blogging)**

If you have a smart phone or a video camera you should be capturing your rise to the top and posting it online so that your adoring fans (at this point your fan base is probably made up of your family and friends) can see how you're doing, looking and feeling about what it is you are doing. Vlogs (also known as video blogs) can be posted on your own website (should you have one) or on 1) youtube.com, 2) vimeo.com, 3) metacafe.com, 4) dailymotion.com, 5) flickr.com, 6) shutterfly.com and even 7) myspace.com (*it's baaaack*).

These are just a few places to upload your Vlog. To find more be sure to do an online search because there are dozens more sites in which you can get your Vlog(s) posted online. *Visit GreenApplesGuide.com for the link to see the vlog for this book.*

(Use this blank space to post/tape business cards, contact notes or create a vision board)

W **Website**

Do you have your personal website? Did you can market and promote yourself through your website? If you have a website, then you are a step ahead of most performers. If you do not have a personal website, then you need to get yourself one. Here are some sites that offer not only website for a reasonable rate or even free but also have templates to help you build your own web image.

1. **Godaddy.com**
2. **Hostmonster.com**
3. **Namecheap.com**
4. **Hostgator.com**
5. **Freewebspace.com**
6. **Justhost.com**
7. **Bluehost.com**
8. **Dreamhost.com**
9. **Simplesite.com**
10. **Rackspace.com**

(Use this blank space to post/tape business cards, contact notes or create a vision board)

> *X* is for e*X*pect Greatness...
>
> **Always eXpect nothing less then greatness from yourself and everyone around you, at all times!** (*Alright, alright, alright... no more of unsolicited advice*)

(Use this blank space to post/tape business cards, contact notes or create a vision board)

Y   YouTube
If you do not have any videos on YouTube, then you need to create some and upload them. Go to youtube.com, sign up for an account, create a few videos and follow the upload instructions given by YouTube. It is that simple to connect yourself to the rest of the world using one of the #1 social media outlets. Please visit GreenApplesGuide.com for links to our YouTube pages.

(Use this blank space to post/tape business cards, contact notes or create a vision board)

Z   Zoom

This popular site enables people and companies to meet up for free videoconferences, classes, seminars, webinars, etc. An interesting tool, which is very useful and used quite frequently in 2020 when the Coronavirus pandemic caused just about everything, across the globe, to close down. Most meetings, casting and other interaction between people are done via Zoom.com.

(Use this blank space to post/tape business cards, contact notes or create a vision board)

SECTION 3:
Personal Planner, Calendar & Journal

2021 Calendar

January
S	M	T	W	T	F	S
					1	2
3	4	5	6	7	8	9
10	11	12	13	14	15	16
17	18	19	20	21	22	23
24	25	26	27	28	29	30
31						

February
S	M	T	W	T	F	S
	1	2	3	4	5	6
7	8	9	10	11	12	13
14	15	16	17	18	19	20
21	22	23	24	25	26	27
28						

March
S	M	T	W	T	F	S
	1	2	3	4	5	6
7	8	9	10	11	12	13
14	15	16	17	18	19	20
21	22	23	24	25	26	27
28	29	30	31			

April
S	M	T	W	T	F	S
				1	2	3
4	5	6	7	8	9	10
11	12	13	14	15	16	17
18	19	20	21	22	23	24
25	26	27	28	29	30	

May
S	M	T	W	T	F	S
						1
2	3	4	5	6	7	8
9	10	11	12	13	14	15
16	17	18	19	20	21	22
23	24	25	26	27	28	29
30	31					

June
S	M	T	W	T	F	S
		1	2	3	4	5
6	7	8	9	10	11	12
13	14	15	16	17	18	19
20	21	22	23	24	25	26
27	28	29	30			

2021 Calendar

July
S	M	T	W	T	F	S
				1	2	3
4	5	6	7	8	9	10
11	12	13	14	15	16	17
18	19	20	21	22	23	24
25	26	27	28	29	30	31

August
S	M	T	W	T	F	S
1	2	3	4	5	6	7
8	9	10	11	12	13	14
15	16	17	18	19	20	21
22	23	24	25	26	27	28
29	30	31				

September
S	M	T	W	T	F	S
			1	2	3	4
5	6	7	8	9	10	11
12	13	14	15	16	17	18
19	20	21	22	23	24	25
26	27	28	29	30		

October
S	M	T	W	T	F	S
					1	2
3	4	5	6	7	8	9
10	11	12	13	14	15	16
17	18	19	20	21	22	23
24	25	26	27	28	29	30
31						

November
S	M	T	W	T	F	S
	1	2	3	4	5	6
7	8	9	10	11	12	13
14	15	16	17	18	19	20
21	22	23	24	25	26	27
28	29	30				

December
S	M	T	W	T	F	S
			1	2	3	4
5	6	7	8	9	10	11
12	13	14	15	16	17	18
19	20	21	22	23	24	25
26	27	28	29	30	31	

Planner/Journal/Notes:

GLOSSARY

      Show business (also known as the "*Business*" or the "*Industry*") is full of colorful terminology, as it pertains to the working Actor. Here is a Glossary of words more commonly used around the Industry. Acting Terms to know for Aspiring Actors. Knowing the terminology used by Hollywood professionals will help you understand what being a professional actor is all about.

A

ACTION – A command given by the director of a film or television show signaling the beginning of a scene. Also means that the camera is rolling.

ACTOR – The person who portrays a character in a recorded or staged production.

ACTORS REEL – Video footage of on-camera productions the actor has been cast in. Can be footage from Films, TV Shows & Commercials.

A.D. (Assistant Director) – is the person who works directly with the director on a film.

AD LIB – Not to be confused with Assistant Director. Ad lib is the adding of dialogue or words (spoken aloud) that are not in the script. Sometimes used when an actor forgets their line.

ADJUSTMENT – A direction or modification an actor makes in the playing of material. They are often instructions given by the director.

AGENT – A person responsible for the professional and contractual business of a performing artist. Agents typically negotiate contracts on behalf of the artist.

ANTAGONIST – The villain or bad guy in a filmed or staged project.

AUDITION – Trying out for a film or stage role. Usually auditions involving reading from the script but can also require improvisation.

B

BACKGROUND – is an "extra" performer, who are on the set, in the background.

BACK TO ONE – The verbal cue for performers to return to the mark where they started the scene.

BEAT – A deliberate, brief pause (short on long) in dialogue or an action.

BLOCKING – Setting up a scene, using physical objects (tables, chairs, etc.) so that the actors or performers can move around them.

BLUE or **GREEN SCREEN** – A blue or green backdrop set up behind performer, used in post-production to superimposed images that aren't there.

BOOKING – The job. You will be 'booked' for a job; this means you are hired. Usually refers to on-camera work.

BOOM MIC – An overhead microphone usually held by Boom Operator (part of the sound department) with a boom pole over and sometimes under the actors.

BREAKDOWN – A written description of a character from a script, usually terms casting notice, used by casting directors to hold auditions and cast a production.

C

CALLBACK – Any follow-up interview or audition.

CALL SHEET – A sheet containing the cast and crew call times for a specific day's shooting. Scene numbers, the expected day's total pages, locations, and production needs are also included.

CALL TIME – For on-camera and theater. This is the time that you are called to be either at the theatre or on the set.

CAMERA READY – This usually means a performer is made up (hair, makeup, clothing, etc.) done and ready to step in front of the camera.

CAST – The group of actors who play all the characters in a show.

CASTING – The process of selecting and hiring actors to play the roles and characters in productions.

CASTING DIRECTOR – Person responsible for choosing performers for consideration by the production team or director to fill roles in a production.

CASTING FACILITY – A studio or space used by one or more casting directors for holding audition sessions.

CASTING NOTICE – The breaking down of characters needed for a production which is published for the public or members of a casting site.

CATTLE CALL – An open audition for performers, without needing a call time or designated time to meet with casting directors.

CENTRAL CONFLICT – The oppositional force between characters that directly affects or motivates the action of the plot.

CHANGES – Different outfits to be worn while performing on set. Production associates will say "w*ear 1, bring 2.*"

CHARACTER – A person, thing, or entity in a story with a set of specific and distinguishing attributes and characteristics.

CINEMATOGRAPHER – Person responsible for capturing, recording or photographing images for a film, through the selection of visual recording devices, camera angles, film stock, lenses, framing, and arrangement of lighting.

CLOSE UP (CU) – Camera term for tight shot of shoulders and face of the performer.

COLD READING – Acting done with the script in your hand, not memorized or partially memorized. First read through or few readings of script.

COOGAN's LAW – A type of bank account (savings) named after child actor Jackie Coogan. This type of account is mandatory for all child performers.

COVERAGE – All camera shots other than the master shot; coverage might include two-shots and close-ups.

CRAFT SERVICES – An area on a production set where snacks and other quickly consumable foods and drinks sit, on a table. Sometimes known simply as "Crafty."

C.S.A. – The Casting Society of America is a professional organization of Casting Directors.

CUE – The action, line, or phrase of dialogue that signals your character to move or speak.

CUT – The verbal cue for the action of the scene to stop. At no time, may an actor call, "cut!"

D

DAY PLAYER – A "Day Player" is a category that the Screen Actors Guild uses for an actor who is contracted to perform for a single day only, as opposed to a longer-term contract.

DEADPAN – A specific type of comedic device in which the performer assumes an expressionless (deadpan) quality to her/his face demonstrating absolutely no emotion or feeling.

DIALECT – A distinctly regional or linguistic speech pattern.

DIALOGUE – The scripted words exchanged by performers.

DIRECTOR – The individual who oversees and directs cast members on a stage or film/TV production set.

DOUBLE – A performer who appears in place of another performer, i.e., as in a stunt.

DOWNSCALE or **UPSCALE** – Term for type of wardrobe or dressed, regular nondescript or casual clothing can be "downscale" while upscale would be the opposite of downscale.

DRESS REHEARSAL – This is when the cast of a production do a read through (aka "run-through") of the script to help with memorizations and build camaraderie.

E

ENSEMBLE ACTING – Acting with a group to unify the members of a cast working together on a production.

ETHNIC TYPES – Referring to the race, nationality, or creed of the talent. Usually describes individuals that are not Caucasian.

ETHNICALLY AMBIGUOUS – Usually means a person's race that is not easily defined by their appearance.

EXT. (Exterior) – A scene to be shot outside.

EXTRA – Background performer, non-principal roles.

EXECUTIVE PRODUCER – A producer who is not involved in any technical aspects of the filmmaking process, but who is still responsible for the overall production.

EXPOSITION – This establishes the setting and characters of the play.

F

FEATURED EXTRA – When an extra is clearly visible on camera and not just a blur in the background.

FI-CORE – 'financial core' status is an option within the Screen Actors Guild (SAG-AFTRA) allowing actors to work both union and non-union jobs.

FIRST A.D. – First Assistant Director (often 1st AD) is a person responsible for the running of the set. Gives instructions to crew and talent, including calling for "first team," "quiet," "rehearsal," and "take five."

FORCED CALL – A call to work less than 12 hours after dismissal on the previous day.

FOURTH WALL – Refers to the imaginary, illusory invisible plane through which the film viewer or audience is thought to look through toward the action.

G

GENRE – The style or theme of a production.

GOLDEN TIME – Refers to the 16th hour of a shooting day, in which performers receive their base pay for each additional hour until released for the day.

GREENROOM – The actors' or guest lounge.

GRIPS – Members of the film crew who are responsible for moving set pieces, lighting equipment, dolly track and other physical movement of equipment.

H

HOLDING – The designated area to which the Extra Performers report and stay while waiting to go on set.

HONEY WAGON – A towed vehicle containing one or more dressing rooms, as well as crew bathrooms.

HOT SET – Any set or location that is being used for filming or taping. Even if the cameras are not rolling, a location can be considered "Hot" if all the props, lights, and camera arrangements are set up and ready. It is important to not disturb anything on a Hot Set as to maintain Continuity.

I

INDUSTRIALS – Industrial Film. Refers to films made for corporations. Training films, product education, Human resource training, etc. Work on industrials often involves memorizing a lot of technical writing.

INT. (Interior) – A scene shot indoors.

'IN' TIME – The actual call time or start time; also, return time from a break.

IMPROVISATION – Acting done without a script; everything is made up on the spot. Often used in rehearsals to strengthen understanding of character. Setting out to do a scene with no pre-planned or written idea. A process leading to spontaneous discovery that allows the actor to find real, organic impulses within themselves.

IMPLUSE – A natural response that an actor responds to in the moment.

INDICATING – Showing what your character is feeling or doing without really feeling or doing, leading to a false and shallow performance.

INNER ACTION – A physical action verb chosen by the actor in the pursuit of an objective. It always begins with the word "to" i.e. to attack, to soothe, to tickle.

INNER MONOLOGUE – A character's active, imaginative inner thoughts while the actor is playing a role.

INSTRUMENT – The actor's collective working of the body, voice, mind, and imagination.

L

LEGAL NAME – This is the name on your birth certificate and usually the name you will receive payments, etc. Stage name is one you create to use on screen.

LONG SHOT (LS) – A camera shot which captures the performer's full body.

M

MAKE-UP – The use of cosmetics to create the appearance of the character during the play. MASKS: A face covering used in theatre to create character or disguise identity.

MARK – (often "*your Mark*") The exact position(s) given to an actor on a set to insure that he/she is in the proper light and camera angle; generally marked on the ground with tape or chalk.

MEAL PENALTY – All film productions should break at least once every six hours to allow for cast and crew meals. If production does not halt for meals at least once every six hours then Union actors and extras are entitled to a "meal penalty" payment for every half hour over the six hours you are not fed.

MEISNER TECHNIQUE – An acting process that uses (among other things) repetitive and in-the-moment exercises first devised by Sanford Meisner of the Group Theatre, to be a "moment-to-moment" spontaneity acting which is being "truthful under imaginary circumstances."

METHOD ACTING – A generic term used to describe the acting philosophy of using personal emotional experiences in acting, devised by Stanislavsky, and can be summed up as: *"Training the subconscious to behave spontaneously."*

MOCUMENTARY – A fictional or farcical production shot with a style that seems like of a documentary or real feel but its scripted or sketched out.

MONOLOGUE – A scene or a portion of a script in which an actor gives a lengthy, unbroken speech without interruption by another character.

MOS (Motion Only Shot) – Any shot without dialogue or sound recording.

N

NAME TALENT ONLY – Meaning only considering celebrity Actors with recognizable names. Stars.

O

OFF BOOK – You have your characters lines completely memorized. Usually you will have a deadline by which you need to be memorized or 'off book'.

ON BOOK – With the script in your hand. Usually refers to the time you are working with the script but not yet memorized.

ON-CAMERA – Refers to anything on camera – tv, film, commercials, industrial film.

ON HOLD – A casting director will put you 'on hold' when you are wanted by the client for the job but not formally hired yet. You may not take other jobs that would conflict with the production dates during this time.

OFF-SCREEN (OS) – Dialogue delivered without being on screen.

OUT OF FRAME – An actor outside the camera range.

"OUT" TIME – The actual time when you are released after you have changed out of wardrobe and make-up. As "In-Time" means the time arriving on set, Out Time is the time you leave the set. Wrapped out (see W for definition of Wrapped).

OVER-THE-SHOULDER – A shot over the shoulder of one actor, focusing entirely on the face and upper torso of the other actor in a scene; generally shot in pairs so both actors' expressions can later be edited together.

P

P.A. – Production Assistant.

PACE – The speed at which you pick up your cue and deliver the next line of your dialogue. Pace can also be the speed that creates a style for the piece.

PAN – A camera shot which sweeps from side-to-side.

PER DIEM – Fee paid by producer on location shoots to compensate performer for expenditures for meals not provided by the producer.

PICK UP – Starting a scene from a place other than the beginning.

PICTURE'S UP – Warning that the sequence of cues to shoot a scene is about to begin.

PILOT – A sample of a television show in which the producers try to sell that show to the networks.

PLOT – The events of a production, from its beginning to end.

POV (Point of View) – A shot that shows the scene through the character's eyes.

PRINCIPAL – A performer with lines.

PRODUCER – A person responsible for the day-to-day decision making on a production.

PSA – Public Service Announcement.

Q-R

REACTION SHOT – The camera shooting a character's emotional or physical response or reaction to something that is happening in the scene.

READ THROUGH – This is a rehearsal, when the actors just read through the script from beginning to end with the director.

REHEARSAL – Practicing or "running lines" with fell cast members of a production.

RESIDUAL – A performance fee paid to actors for rebroadcast of a commercial, film or TV program. Tracking done by various actor Unions.

RESUME – A list of production credits, usually attached to or accompanied by a headshot.

ROLLING – The verbal command given by the director to start rolling the camera and begin filming action on the production set.

RUSH CALL – Last minute booking of an actor or extra.

S

SCRIPT – The written form of a screenplay, teleplay, radio or stage play.

SECOND ASSISTANT DIRECTOR (2nd AD) – Often two or three on a set, they handle checking in the talent, insuring proper paperwork is filed, distribute script revisions.

SET – The location where a production will be filmed.

SFX – Sound effects.

SIDES – Pages or scenes from a script.

SIGN-IN SHEET – A sheet at the casting office where talent will sign their Name, Agency, Phone number and time arrived to the casting office.

SLATE – The verbal identification of a performer in a taped audition (e.g., "Slate your name!"), in which they give names, location and/or other pertinent information.

STAND-INS – Extra Performers used as substitutes for featured players, for the purpose of setting lights and rehearsing camera moves; also known as the second team.

SUBMISSION – An actor's or agent's suggestion to a casting director for a role in a certain production.

T

TABLE-READ – A film, television or theatre script reading usually held around a table.

TAFT-HARTLEY – Non-union actors who work their first union job and any other jobs within a 30-day period of the first booking without having to join the union will be able to join the union. Also, that actor should not work any union job after the 30-day period without joining the union.

TAG LINE – A clever phrase or short sentence to memorably characterize a film, and tease and attract potential viewers, or sell the project.

TAKE(S) – This term references shots "taken" or printed for future viewing and/or editing.

TAKE 5 – The announcement of a five-minute breaks.

TRADE PAPERS ("*TRADES*") – The newspapers and periodicals such as the Hollywood Reporter and Variety that specifically feature information on the entertainment industry.

TREATMENT – A detailed outline of the plot, characters, high points of a production.

TRIPLE THREAT – Refers to an performer who has more than one talent or skill (i.e., sing, dance and act OR act, write and produce OR even write, produce and direct).

TURNAROUND – (a) The number of hours between dismissal one day and call time the next day. (b) To shoot a scene from another direction.

TYPECAST – A performer who becomes strongly identified with a specific character and are always viewed in that light.

U

UNDER 5 – An actor whose character has fewer than five lines of dialogue in a production.

UNDERSTUDY – Actor hired to perform in a show if the actor originally cast in the role is sick or unable to perform that night. Usually occurs in stage/theatre.

V

V.O. (Voice-Over) - Off-camera voice coming from an actor not in the frame or from a secondary source (speakerphone, answering machine, or vocals laid over moving picture).

VIDEO VILLAGE – The area where all of the camera shots are fed into video monitors, allowing the director to get an accurate view of every shot.

VOUCHER – Time slip with all pertinent information needed for getting paid properly.

W – X – Y – Z

WALK-ON – A minor role consisting of a single, brief appearance on the screen, usually not appearing in the credits and without dialogue; contrast with extras, bit parts, and non-speaking roles.

WARDROBE – The clothing a performer wears on camera.

WARDROBE ALLOWANCE – A maintenance fee paid to on-camera talent for the use (and dry cleaning) of talent's own clothing.

WARDROBE FITTING – A session held prior to production to prepare a performer's costumes.

"WEATHER PERMIT" CALL – Due to weather conditions, the production company has the option to release an actor four hours after the call time (if the camera has not started to roll) with a reduced rate of pay for the day.

W/N – Will Notify. A notation on a call sheet that tells the actor that he/she will probably work that day but the specific time has not yet been decided.

WRAP (WRAPPED or **WRAP OUT)** – The completion of a day's filming or of the entire production.

OTHER TERMS

8×10 – Commonly used size of a performer's Headshot/photos. Another term for headshot. Black and white was the standard in the old days, today headshots are in color.

18-TO-PLAY-YOUNGER – A performer legally 18 years old, who can convincingly be cast as a younger age.

TALENT UNIONS

AEA – Actors' Equity Association; also called "Equity". This is the union most theatre/stage talent are members of. The sister union to SAG-AFTRA.

AFTRA – American Federation of TV and Radio Artists (the union). Covers radio, vocal recording and soap operas. Now merged with SAG (screen Actors Guild) renamed to SAG-AFTRA.

ACTRA – Alliance of Canadian Cinema Television and Radio Artists.

SAG: Screen Actors Guild.

SAG-AFTRA: The uniting of the SAG and AFTRA unions.

Jot down any other Terms you may come across in Hollywood:

That's A *Wrap*... For This Book

However, it's just beginning for you and your mission of Breaking into Hollywood!

It's time to ask yourself...

AM I READY?

If your answer is no, then ask yourself ... *IF NOT NOW, WHEN??*

This is your call to duty! Time to GRIND and make yourself into the success story you know you have the potential to be! Whether you are already hustling every day to make your dreams a reality or you're just in the "*I'm going to do it one of these days*" stages. There is never a better time than right now to get your HUSTLE and GRIND on!!!

You MUST hustle every day until you can sit back and see what you've worked so hard and/or so long for. SUCCESS! The time is now to make it happen!!!

Once you find your way into Hollywood and want to learn things like how to become a producer or start your own entertainment related business, we have the following books coming down the pipeline:

WHO READY: *To Boss Up on Hollywood.*
(learn the ABCs & 123s of becoming a Self-Producing Performer in this book)

THE B.O.S.$ THEORY
(a how-to/self-help business start-up workbook)

ABOUT THE AUTHOR

MS Blackwell went to college to get a degree in political science and pursue a career in law but ended-up becoming a writer, independent producer, performer and entrepreneur, who started producing projects for herself and other artists. Part of her business was a small school she named the Hollywood Performance Academy (visit HollywoodBackdoor.com), which provided an alternative approach to breaking into the entertainment business, also known as *Hollywood* or the *Industry* or even just the *Business*.

The first edition or version of the **ABCs & 123s of Breaking into Hollywood** book (which was simply title the *GreenApples Guide to Breaking into Hollywood: The ABCs and 123s for making it happen*) was not actually published, officially. It was a manual Coach Michelle put together and handed out during her classes from 2007-2014. Then Coach decided to publish and sell the book to people who attended her classes and those who just needed a little help figuring out how to break into Hollywood.

When Covid-19 hit and the world shut down, Coach Michelle took her classes and workshops online (again visit HollywoodBackdoor.com for a list of classes) and decided to revise and publish an updated version of this book, which is what you currently have in your hand. With this book she has made lots of changes, updates and additions to better assist aspiring artists. It's time to learn and practice the **ABCs & 123s of Breaking into Hollywood**!!

www.ingramcontent.com/pod-product-compliance
Lightning Source LLC
Chambersburg PA
CBHW081509080526
44589CB00017B/2700